DISCLAIMER

By reading this disclaimer, you fully accept the terms of this disclaimer. If you are not in agreement with this disclaimer, please do not order or read this book. The content of this book is provided for information and educational purposes only.

Table of Contents

AIR PLANTS OVERVIEW

Air plants are finding a place in home decor. Care is not difficult if you understand how they grow in their natural environment. Very unique plants any one can ever come across are Air plants (Tillandsia) appears in 450 over different varieties. I fell in love with Air Plants the very first time I beheld one! I just couldn't figure out how it was thriving, just clinging to that tree. Since then, I have found out, through research and personal experience, exactly how that plant maintained life. And I found out a lot of other things about them, as well! They are classified under the bromeliad family which covers a wide variety of 3,475 mainly tropical plant species this means that air plants are related to pineapples! Really! They can be found in different regions that range from the top of Argentina to the southern US. The two main types of air plants are xeric and mesic. Xeric Tillandsia lives in desert climates and can survive with less water and more sun than their tropical counterparts (mesic Tillandsia).

Air plants lock their roots to trees, rocks, and other plants, and absorb water that accumulates at their base. For instance, they live in a tropical forest in the trees that collect humidity and water from the branches of the trees. Due to their acclimation to the rainforest and warm desert weather, they prefer temperatures in the range of 50–90° F (10–32° C). Mesic Tillandsia prefers humid air while xeric Tillandsia prefers arid air. If you don't live in an area that boasts their preferred conditions, no need to worry there are ways to replicate that environment and air plants are fairly resilient.

They come in a large variety of sizes and colors. Air plant varieties range in size from two inches to seven feet. The varieties that are frequently found in stores are typically two to five inches in size. There are varieties that bloom flowers but this usually signals that the plant is near the end of its life cycle. Before air plants die they release pups (baby air plants) that grow up to be just like the original.

Air plants usually only bloom once. The flowers can last from 2 weeks to a year depending on the type of air crop. This flower appears in a variety of colors, including purple, pink, yellow, orange and red. At the end of the winter, the air plants bloom and go well the same way into the spring.

Outdoor air plants may become pollinated while in bloom. If this happens, the seed pods are going to be made. Such pods contain a lot of small seeds that spread naturally in the wind. The air crop from these seeds can be cultivated, but it takes 2 to 4 years and is difficult to grow. The crop has a different way of replicating it. This is originally vegetative and begins when small baby plants (called pups) are produced around the base. When mature, depending on the species, it takes a variable amount of time; it can be removed and converted to a new air seed. Instead, a larger plant may be left attached to the adult. The pups will, in turn, mature into adults, bloom and make their own pups. Usually, air plants have been living for about 8 years.

Before I started gardening, Air plant was the first plant I tried to grow. They're incredibly tough and quite easy to grow, which is the perfect combination for beginners. You still have to keep an eye on them, however. This book is just the platform for you starters to learn greatly about Air Plants.

You will learn how to build the ideal atmosphere for your air plant to thrive in this book, how to mount and divide it, how to water and feed it, and finally how to deal with pests and diseases.

What are Air Plants?

Air plants or Aerial plants are plants whose roots are above the ground. Most of them are hung in pots that have little or no soil at all. Basically they can grow without soil. There are numerous forms of aerial crop. Some of them, like the spider plant, still have the typical terrestrial roots. Plants such as these simply have aerial roots as additional parts; for the collection of nutrients they do not rely entirely on them. Others, however, have completely abandoned soil dependence. Called epiphytes, they have established their roots that do not need the soil medium and receive the nutrients to survive from the air while relying instead on support from a third-party crop.

Due to the ease of setting up, Air plants (Tillandsia) have become hugely popular and most often sought after by indoor gardeners. Most of these plants are also best placed in areas where one can see them easily, providing metaphorically and literally a relaxing and pleasant atmosphere. Some air plants have several water-filtering properties, which is the number one reason anyone can identify these plants actively. You're definitely going to want these cool little greens around. There are many air plants that you can find and add to your home!

Air Plant Taxonomy

Plants are classified into a family. Families are then broken up into divisions based on similarities and differences. These divisions are called genuses. Within the genus are more subgroups called species. (There are more groups within the plant naming hierarchy, but we won't worry about those.) The family to which air plants are classified is as follows: Family: Bromeliad>Genus: Tillandsia>Species: include the various types of Tillandsias

Air Plants and Epiphytes

The term epiphytes describes plants that live on other plants, or rocks, or whatever else they can latch onto for support, but are not parasitic. They do not take nutrients from the host plant. Epiphytes do not have typical root systems that burrow into soil to absorb nutrients.

Epiphyte is a description, not a classification. Although both air plants and orchids are epiphytes they belong to different families. Tillandsia belongs to the bromeliad family, while orchids are part of the orchidaceae family. Ferns and mosses are other examples of plants that are also epiphytes that belong to other families.

The function of tillandsia roots is to anchor them to a host. They do not absorb any water or other nutrients through their roots. In fact, tillandsia roots can be cut off at the base of the plant without any harm to the plant. When you purchase a tillandsia their roots will have already been trimmed off. Over time the roots will begin to grow again. If you think the roots are a bit unsightly, trim them off.

Trichomes

Rather than roots, air plant leaves are covered with trichomes, tiny sponge-like cells that absorb water and nutrients for the plant. And that's not all; trichomes perform another function for the plant: sun protection. Tillandsias from more sunny climates sport more trichomes, while those from shadier locations have fewer, less visible trichomes.

Xeric and Mesic

Tillandsias that come from harsher, dryer climates with more pronounced trichomes revealing a more silvery appearance with stiffer leaves are known as xeric. Tillandsia that originate from more tropical climates are known as mesic. These plants are less silvery and softer to the touch than xeric tillandsia. Their trichomes are less pronounced and may even be microscopic.

The bottom line here is that xeric tillandsia can handle more intense sun and are more drought tolerant, while mesic tillandsia don't have the same high light requirements as do the xeric plants.

While it is useful to know which types of air plants you own, you can certainly grow both mesic and xeric varieties, no matter where you live. Also there are some air plants that don't fall neatly into either category and are known as semi-mesic. Another tillandsia subgroup is called hydric. These plants live in or around water and do not thrive in a home environment and aren't readily available.

Infinite Benefits of Air Plants

Air Plants are colorful, easy to care for, exotic and affordable. Due to the many positive attributes of Air Plants, they are becoming more and more popular, making them perfect for urban setting, including apartments, homes, offices, restaurants and store displays. Looking for Holiday Gifts that are truly unique, exotic and really cool? Give a gift that keeps on giving.

Interior Decoration

Air plants decorate your interior to make it look more elegant and lovely. Colorful ones will boost your home space. You can put them in the kitchen to add a natural appearance. Instead, to compliment your furniture, you can place it in your sitting room. You can customize it to suit any style or design. You can put them in and hang them in classy bottle terrariums, for example. Your house is going to look brand new and charming. It creates a wonderful environment for visitors and the whole family.

They bloom and produce arrays of colors such as red, purple, yellow, orange and magenta. They get meticulously attractive when they blossom and produce such notable colors. You can blend the colors to get the most appealing décor that you fancy.

Enhance Air Supply

As the name suggests, if you grow them indoors, there will be transfer of oxygen and carbon dioxide, the air plants will add oxygen. It means you can never run out of the water at any moment. Plants take carbon dioxide you release. As a result, you will supply fresh air on a regular basis. In addition, it's all natural and non-toxic. Typically, many houses do not have adequate ventilation. You can breathe in with water plants; enough air every day.

Reduce Allergies

Most people in the United States of America suffer from allergies and asthma. Air plants contain all allergens to prevent sneezing, watery eyes and coughing. We've got trichomes that can trap allergy-causing dust and pollen. So the air is going to get the cleaning it needs. Air plants serve as defenses against all kinds of irritants. Air fresheners, candles, good perfumes and aerosol products are also included. Trichomes are about to get rid of them and purify the water.

Contribute to Positive Energy

When you feel sad or miserable most of the time, having air plants around brings positive vibe. To control stress and anger, they have been scientifically proven. It also regulates depression and mood swings. That's why you'll feel much happier and happier. When you have air plants in your bedroom or sitting room, you'll be in high spirits. They're still supplying you with energy so you don't get tired. It makes you involved and willing to deal with any task you need to accomplish. Therefore, you're not going to delay significant, worthwhile activities. Finally, as you do your daily duties, you will be more relaxcd and calm. Above all, they act as stress relievers which will make life more bearable. You will feel hopeful and yearn for a better tomorrow.

Refine The Air

Air plants take all of the house's carbon dioxide from various sources. They draw all of the air's dust, mold, bacteria, and humidity. It detoxifies the air that leans no unturned rock. As a consequence, you can breathe in safe substance-free air. Air plants give you the best chance to inhale country air. That form of air has no toxins in garden-fresh oxygen. For order to have a safe respiratory system, you should invest for air plants.

Improve Productivity

If you lack focus and concentration, then air plants are your best solution. They will boost your productivity levels and ensure that you achieve all your objectives and goals. You should place some air plants at your desk or at home in your study room. In a short time, you will find yourself performing tasks. You can come up with brilliant ideas, too, as you work. To top it up, you can make sound and quality decisions with a straight mind. The science behind it is that there is less carbon dioxide in the air. Clean air means that your mind is also clear about how you should see things in the right way.

Manages High Blood Pressure

You're going to be impressed to hear that the air plants are controlling blood pressure. As mentioned earlier, it lowers stress levels. This, in turn, translates into stable blood pressure. It will not shoot up when you are agitated because the air plant will calm you down. They are therefore important for people with high blood pressure. You're not going to have to prepare a concoction to be better. All you need to do is inhale the awesome air produced by the amazing plants. Then you'll feel like you've been meditating straight for five hours.

Flexible and Versatile

You don't have to choose a perfect spot to grow air plants; they can adapt to any room. In that case, by putting them in different containers, you can customize the theme. They are also abundant in glasses or bottles. In bowls or concrete pots, you can also grow them. Since they don't need soil for growth, the magic can be achieved by any ravishing owner. You can even switch them from room to room. They're not heavy, so they're super flexible.

Durable

Air plants are immune to pathogens and insects that are susceptible to them. We're going to last longer with the right amount of sunlight and air. They're not going to wither and they're going to die off easily. You can rely on them to support you for a lifetime. All you need to do is show them basic care, and they're always going to look the best. Air babies growing from the main plant underscore the advantages of air plants. You can move them to another container to allow them to continue to develop.

Most Popular Types of Air Plants

In addition to their variance in size, they come in a vast variety of color combinations. You can find pastel green plants and other bright types that feature fiery reds, pinks and purples. As mentioned above there are two main air plant categories, xeric and mesic. Xeric air plants are characterized by muted silver and green color tones and a fuzzy texture. Mesic air plants have a smoother texture and brighter colors.

Tillandsia Cyanea (Pink Quill)

The pink quill air plant is named for its distinct bright pink feather-like bloom. Another thing that makes the pink quill plant unique is that it can grow in soil and does just as well being grown in either soil or in the air. The pretty pink quill will occasionally have flowers bloom on it, although the flowers only last a couple of days and the quill can only support about two flowers at a time.

Tillandsia Usneoides (Spanish Moss)

Spanish moss looks quite different from the other air plant varieties with its long stringy texture. In its natural environment, the plant drapes over tree branches, creating a gorgeous ethereal effect. Spanish moss isn't Spanish. It got its nickname from

French explorers who thought it looked like a Spanish Conquistador's beard.

Tillandsia Bulbosa

The bulbosa's lanky bracts create a stark contrast to the large bulbous roots. If grown outdoors, this plant develops a symbiotic relationship with ants. The ants find shelter in the bulbs and the plant feeds on the ant's waste. As an added bonus, this variety does well in low-light conditions. A downside of Tillandsia bulbosoa is that water can get trapped in the base easily and lead to root rot if it's not dried properly after being watered.

Tillandsia Aeranthos Bergeri

This variety blooms every spring, revealing gorgeous pink and purple flowers. Tillandsia aeranthos bergeri grows pups very quickly, faster than other varieties, so it's a great option for someone who loves to propagate their plants. It's also a bigger air plant variety compared to other Tillandsia houseplant varieties, they can grow to about six to nine inches tall.

Tillandsia Ionantha (fuego)

Fuego air plants are small but mighty at two inches tall. What they lack in height is made up for in color these plants have stunning bright red and orange hues to them. They hail from Mexico and South America in humid warm forests, so they love when their caretakers can mimic this environment.

Amazing Things Nobody Tells You about Air Plants

I've never met an air plant that I didn't think was adorable. Tillandsias are the tribbles of houseplants no matter whether a variety is fuzzy, furry, spiky, rounded, or has long, trailing foliage that looks like a ponytail, it's irresistible.

With nearly 600 known varieties of these low-maintenance houseplants which call tropical climates home, there's an air plant to make any houseplant collector happy. But Tillandsias can be tricky, too. They have a few secrets of their own. Learn them, and your air plants will thrive.

1. An air plant will not grow in soil. Don't even try it.

Unlike plants that absorb nutrients and water through their root systems, Air Plants have specialized cells called trichomes over their entire surface to get the job done.

The function of these trichomes is to collect ambient moisture, particles from decaying plants and bits of insect matter from the air. The Air Plant utilizes this hydration and nutrition internally. At night, the pores of the Air plant open to allow for the process of photosynthesis, and the plant releases oxygen into the air.

Outdoor Air Plants need little human interaction (depending on the climate) to flourish, but indoor Air Plants are 100% dependant on their humans for survival. Indoor plants will clean the air in your home using their Trichomes, but will still need regular watering, occasional feedings (via fertilizer) and careful observation to ensure they are receiving adequate lighting.

2. Air plants use roots to attach themselves to things (rather than to absorb nutrients).

You can mount a tillandsia like a trophy to hang on a wall or arrange several together in a single planter suspended from the ceiling.

3. Air Plants Have a Long History

No one can say when the first Air Plants were "discovered". Likely they have been around as long as any other plant that grows naturally in humid and warm environments. Also likely that there were more of them once before man began to develop forests into cities!

In nature, Air Plants live in shade near a forest's "ceiling" to receive the light they need to promote life. Their roots anchor them to trees, and their leaves grow in a funnel shape to help pull in and retain water from rains.

We do know that the Genus of the most common variety of Air Plants, Tillandsia, was named in the 1600s by Carl Linnaeus. He named it after the Swedish physician and botanist Dr. Elias Tillandz.

4. Air Plants are Slow Growers

If you're looking for large Air Plants to decorate your space, I'll save you some time and frustration by telling you to purchase large ones, rather than waiting for small ones to grow large.

The most common and best-selling Air Plants can triple in size over their life-span, but will always fit in the palm of your hand.

An Air Plant that is considered by standards to be "large" is rarely over 10 inches in diameter, like this Tillandsia Xerographica, whose name in Greek means "dry writing"

Some other large Air Plants varieties are Bulbosa, Caput Medusa, Juncea and Circinata.

6. Air plants need sunlight like any other plants.

It's a mistake to treat your air plant as if it's a decorative object rather than a living thing. Just because it's amiable enough to live in a bowl or on a bookshelf without benefit of soil doesn't mean it can survive without air, light or water. Air plants like several hours a day of bright, indirect light.

7. Air plants can't live on air alone.

Air plants get nutrition by absorbing water through their leaves. A good rule of thumb is to water an air plant once a week. Of course, bend the rule based on the conditions in your own home. If the air in your home is particularly dry, water an air plant more often (every five days) and in a humid environment, water tillandsias every ten days.

8. Air plants will tell you when you they need more or less water.

Your air plant will let you know if it needs water more often (the tips of its leaves will turn brown and curl) or if you are over-watering it (its leaves may turn brown or start to look soggy). Be careful if it turns black, that means it's rotted and beyond saving.

9. Etsy is a great place to shop for well-priced or unusual varieties of air plants.

Many Etsy sellers propagate their own air plants, and sell unusual varieties such as fuzzy white Tectorums. Because tillandsias are sturdy, self-contained plants that don't require soil, they are easy to ship without bruising or harm.

10. You're not the only one having a hard time identifying your Tillandsia varieties.

With more than 550 varieties of known air plants, you'd be hard-pressed under any circumstances to keep them straight. Complicating matters, air plant breeders cross varieties so frequently that you are never really going to see two air plants that are identical

To complicate matters further two plants of the same variety may look completely different, depending on factors such as climate. The same type will look different in Florida and in California

11. An air plant may flower, but only once in its lifetime.

Depending on the species, these blossoms last from a few days to a few months, and can be a whole variety of beautiful bright colors, like pink, red and purple. Flowering is the peak of the air plant life cycle, but also marks the beginning of the plant's old age after it flowers, the plant will eventually die.

12. Propagate an air plant by harvesting its "pups."

Just before, during or after flowering, depending on the species, your air plant will reproduce by sending out from two to eight 'pups'. These baby air plants, which start out very small, will eventually grow into their own mother plants. Pups can safely be separated from the mother plant when they're about ⅓ to ½ its size.

13. Air plants come from tropical climes and will appreciate warm temperatures in your home.

The happiest air plants live in temperatures that range from 50 to 90 degrees Fahrenheit. They will thrive with temperature fluctuations a 10-degree drop that mimics the conditions at nightfall in the Central American regions they call home is ideal.

14. Air Plants can Change Colors

Most Air plants start out with varying shades of green, but as they near their flowering stage, those leaves can begin to change colors! Depending on the variety of Air plant, you'll see colors like yellow, red, magenta, purple or orange, not just on the blossom, but on the leaves as well. The colors are rich and vibrant, too!

15. Imports are Strictly Governed in Some Countries

No Air Plants are native to Australia, and plant nurseries there had been dependant upon imports for all their Air Plants. As of 2016, the Australian Government has severely restricted the import of All Plants, including Air Plants, from the United States and Europe, the two biggest exporters.

This move was made in an effort to stop the spread of an airborne pathogen called Xylella, which can be next to impossible to eradicate. The only option to obtain Air plants in Australia now is to grow them from seed, which is a very long process. Many Air Plant nurseries there were closed down by this governing, and the economic impact hit Australia hard.

16. Air Plants are Excellent for Children to Grow

Children love to nourish things, don't they? It's a habit we'd do well to encourage! Children are also easily distracted, though, and can flit from one project to the next effortlessly. Some adults can too, LOL!

Air Plants are great for children, because of their low maintenance and stamina for survival. They will bring a child's room to life, can be displayed in a plethora of creative ways, and clean the air of the room they're in!

I would encourage you to encourage your child to be a nurturing human by helping him place Air plants around his room. Have fun! Get creative! Get silly! You'll be growing more than Air Plants with your child, you'll be growing memories! And if he forgets to water the plant on occasion, chances are the plant will still be savable. You just can't go wrong.

17. No Air Plant Variety is Toxic to Pets or Children

If your pet, or even your toddler, is a plant nibbler, you take extra caution with which plants you display in your home, as well you should. I know, because my kitty nibbles all live plants as if to see how much fun they might be!

You'll be relieved; I am sure, to learn that No Variety of Air Plant is Toxic to living things. Should a living thing do some nibbling, the Air plant will suffer, and not the living thing that nibbled.

You may also be relieved to learn that no reports have ever been made of a human or animal being allergic to Air Plants. Even people with severe asthma can breathe easy amid Air plants. Pollen isn't an issue, either. Rather, Air plants have properties used to inhibit pollen-related allergies!

18. Air Plants Allow People with Mysophobia to Enjoy Live Plants

Mysophobia is the scientific name for people who have an extraordinary fear of germs. For years, many who have desired to enjoy living plants in their home were unable, due to their concerns about what the soil may contain. Understandably so, considering that dirt is dirty!

Air Plants are a way to enjoy bringing that pop of life indoors for anyone, without bringing messy soil inside!

19. Air Plants are good for People Who Travel Often

These days, we are more connected to the world than at any other time in history. For this reason, many jobs require travel for their employees. This travel can be a hindrance to those who enjoy having a plethora of house plants to tend. For those who travel frequently, Air plants offer an excellent solution to those "gardening blues"!

Both indoor and outdoor Air plants that have sufficient lighting and moisture can be left unattended for longer periods of time than most soil-dependant plants. This is, of course, with the caveat that indoor Air Plants do receive proper care at regular intervals between travels.

20. A Failing Air plant can be Easily Revived

Unless your Air plant had had all its leaves fall off or has been through a deep freeze, reviving an Ailing

Air Plant is relatively simple! If you see browning tips on your Air plant, yellowing leaves, wilting or leaves that begin to curve inward, a little tender loving care will bring the plant back to its full splendor!

The Perfect Air Plant Care Environment

Air plants, like most other plants, are very similar in nature. They will thrive in the right environment. Luckily, as gardeners, we have the power to control some variables to help create the perfect environment. Light, air circulation, temperature and humidity are the factors that need to be taken into account.

Light

Air plants are no different from all plants. They need light, but they definitely need the right amount of light. For general guidelines, plants with thicker, tougher, grayish leaves may be exposed to lighter than those with thinner, grayish / green leaves.

Plants for indoor air must be located in an environment that receives (if possible) organic, clear, diffused light. It should be about 3 to 5 inches from the source of light. Both make excellent choices as a light source including filtered sunlight as a window, sky light or clear glass gate. In a shaded area, outdoor air plants should be kept close enough to natural light. Nonetheless, the air plant should not get too much heat, as in the long run it will be hurt. Some early morning or late afternoon sun, coupled with high humidity, may be appropriate.

Air plants can also grow in artificial lights, including fluorescent lights or LEDs. The air plant should be mounted around 10-30 inches from the light source. Approximately twelve hours of light per day must be received by an air plant growing under artificial light. Never use halogen or incandescent lights because they generate too much heat and, if they are too close to the light source, they will eventually kill the crop.

Air Circulation

It is necessary to place the air plants in an environment with adequate water circulation. This is attributable to two primary factors. Next, the plant can draw nutrients from the soil through its trichomes. Second, after irrigation, moving air plays a critical role in cooling the plant. The plant should dry out properly, especially near the bottom of the plant where all the leaves are gathered. Any water left here is going to start rotting the crop. During times of extreme weather, air movement also helps to keep an air plant cooler.

Air circulation arrears may also allow pests to invade the air crop.

Air movement can come from a variety of sources. For indoor plants, position the air plant in an area where there is a natural movement of air in the house. It may come from an open window or even a draught that passes through the house, allowing air to circulate when other windows and doors are closed. Of course, air circulation is generated by a natural source, the wind, for outdoor air plants.

Temperature

Air plants grow in the wild in a variety of temperatures and the same applies to your home air plants. A better idea is to keep them in an environment that, if possible, has a temperature between 50 and 90 degrees Fahrenheit with no more than a 10 degree fall at night. If kept in this distance, air plants can definitely thrive. They can be kept at higher temperatures but need more regular watering.

Cold temperatures have been detrimental to the health of the air plant for a long period of time. Air plants can tolerate exposure to light frost, but they will be harmed. Nevertheless, if they are exposed for a long time, they will die.

Humidity

That may be essential. Usually, air plants that are dark to light green will need more regular water and a higher level of humidity than gray varieties.

If you can provide once or twice a week with a mist / soak, you should be fine, and humidity can be largely ignored. If watering, however, is often a struggle for you, then the humidity must be reasonably high as a compromise.

Watering

There are two main ways to irrigate the air plants. The first one sprays the leaves with a mystery two or three times a week. This is very useful when your plant is fixed in place, such as being placed on a wall, or it's too hard to try the next step.

The second option is to dunk your Air Plant in a container of room temperature water. Some people will say a dunk isn't enough and instead you'll need to soak the plant in the container for half hour or longer.

I don't necessarily disagree with this, particularly if you live in a very dry area, or if your plant is extremely dehydrated. But soaking in this way on a daily basis makes it difficult and much more time consuming to take care of these plants than it really needs to be.

Instead, I find that they are perfectly content and still get an efficient watering by dunking in the tub for no more than 15 seconds before extracting them and shaking off the excess water.

What's important here is to shake off any excess water and leaving enough time for the plant to fully dry before night falls and the temperatures drop. If there is too much moisture around the plant and it gets cold then there is potential for rotting to occur. So in general try and water in the morning rather than late in the evening.

Feeding

Feeding at least a few times a year is a good idea, as it will give you a solid, safe Air Plant in the long run. You might use a specialty bromeliad, cactus or orchid feed, or even a normal houseplant fertiliser diluted to half the intensity (they don't need much). Avoid fertilizers containing boron, copper or zinc.

The only catch is to avoid fertilizers containing boron, copper or zinc, as all three metals are toxic to the majority of Tillandsias, including Air Plants.

The feed can then be applied to the leaves in the mister spray or in the container of water if you're dunking / soaking your plant.

Watering and Fertilizing

The appearance of the leaves of your air plant will send you hints as to how to take care of it.

Fuzzy leaves with feathery, black, silvery and dusty coatings suggest xeric types from warm, dry climates where precipitation is less frequent. Their pronounced trichomes, when it rains, collect full water and keep it in the dry season. They need watering only once or twice a week and they can handle more sun.

Smooth, glossy leaves are most commonly found in the mesic types of shaded, humid rain and cloud forest where ample water is collected. These have less pronounced trichomes and less drying and hot sunshine coverage. They like to drink more often than not.

Depending on the plant, its location and your own preferences, the best way to water your air crop. Using room temperature tap and rainwater but never soften water because your plants may be harmed by the salt in it.

Choose the most convenient method for you and your plants:

• Misting is ideal for plants inside globes or displays, especially for people who want to communicate with their plants on a regular basis. Mist three to seven days a week, depending on the type of plant, and seek to wet all surfaces.

• Dunking is good for plants that are attached to wood or freestanding, as well as those with dense or very curly leaves that are hard to mist thoroughly. Dip the whole plant briefly into a pan of water or a freshwater fish tank, or put under a running faucet. Use this method two to four times per week for mesic types and once a week for xeric types.

- Soaking helps revive dry plants. Submerge the whole plant for 1 to 3 hours. Use this method once a week or after a period of neglect.

Shake the excess after watering so that there is no standing water in the middle of it. Let the plants dry in a well-ventilated area so that they do not remain damp. Water is more common in warm, hot and desert climates, and less frequently in cold, rainy weather. Tip: Avoid placing them in mud when "planting" that stays damp, which can cause air plants to rot.

Use a water-soluble orchid or tillandsia fertilizer to fertilize air plants once or twice a month, following product dilution instructions. Use the form of misting and dunking. There is no urea nitrogen in these special fertilizers, which air plants cannot use. Tip: If your plant is very dry, soak it first, then fertilize it the next day.

Air Plant Fertilizer & Nutritional Needs

Humans eat large quantities of food and drink to support their lives. Air plants have adapted to do the same in such a way that they can live and thrive in extreme environments. Unique evolutionary adaptations have allowed Tillandsia to be able to control and store nutrients and moisture.

Because air plants come from different ecological climates, we will break them down into two different climate groups: Xeric and Mesic. Xeric tillandsia, like Xerographica and Harisii, live in dry, drought prone climates where water can be scarce for long periods of time. Mesic tillandsia, like Bulbosa Belize and Streptophylla, live in wetter climates that get more regular rain, fog or mist.

Because these are vastly different environments, tillandsia have evolved in different ways.

Transporting Nutrients from Air to Plant

The plant structure for both types of plants has identical components. They all have an epidermis and a hypodermis that make up their skin. The epidermis is the outer skin that protects the water-storing hypodermis. Xeric plants have to store more water like camel than mesic plants, so that they typically have thicker hypodermis. Most of the air plants in commercial production today fall under the xeric climate group. Xeric tillandsia also has more trichomes than her mesic brothers and sisters, as they have to rely more on them for the collection of water and food. Mesic tillandsia have fewer trichomes that are more spread out because they rely more on catching water and nutrient-rich detritus in their axils (spaces between leaves at the base of the plants.) Nutrients and moisture are then transported throughout the plant using very complex "vascular" systems. These distinct differences exemplify the amazing adaptations that have allowed air plants to live in challenging and ever-changing climates.

How they process the Food & Water

Like other plants, Tillandsia need energy to maintain and create new plants cells that make up the body of the plant. Photosynthesis is a method used by most plants to convert inorganic substances like sunlight, water, CO_2 and minerals into energy. Photosynthetically Active Radiation or PAR is taken in through the plant's skin cells and through a complex process converts it to sugars. Such sugars can be broken down, processed and used to energize the plant. Energy is used to produce new leaves to keep them alive. Extra energy is required to blossom or replicate. If you live in wild nutrients and minerals, leave the leaves, the wood or the rock on which the plants grow. Water takes these nutrients to the plant where they are absorbed. When in a house or a greenhouse this system is 100% in motion but we can supplement the process with fertilizer.

What the plant need to Thrive

Air plants are thirsty for nitrogen, potassium and phosphorus, among other minerals. Standard plant fertilizers have these in it, but not in the right shape or ratio. For most plants, the nitrogen fertilizer portion is broken down in the soil to allow plants to absorb it. Air plants do not live in soil, so they have to receive nitrogen in a particular way. Ammonia and Nitrate Nitrogens can be consumed immediately and without being broken down by soil. Only Epiphyte fertilizers have the right amount of minerals that directly support air plants.

Air Plant Propagation, Division, & Cultivation

Everyone is always excited to hear that their new air plants will eventually begin growing small baby air plants called "pups." Pup production is the easiest way to propagate their air plants for air plant hobbyists and nurserymen alike. Pups will always grow crops that have the same characteristics as the mother plant. After blooming, tillandsia produces small seeds, but seed germination production involves a lot of patience and as pollination requires other air plants, germinated plants may not be true to the species.

Pup production ensues shortly after an air plant's first bloom cycle. Depending on the species, an air plant can take 6 months to several years to produce its first bloom. Most of the plants offered in our store will arrive matured, and should bloom within 6 months of you receiving them. After blooming, you will begin to notice small growth nodes at the bottom of the original plant. When you see the small pups, continue to take care of the mother plant normally for the next few months. Take care to not damage the pups as they are very delicate when they first start growing.

Once the pups are between a quarter to half the size of the mother plant, they are ready to be separated. To ensure a clean cut, garden shears or a sharp kitchen knife are preferred. Gently lay the mother plant on its side and cut away the pups. Congratulations! You can now start your very own air plant farm! After their initial separation, it's best to allow the separation point on both the mother and newly-separated pup to "harden off" for a few days. Leave the plants to rest and for the cut to dry off before placing back inside terrariums or watering the plants. This will discourage bacterial growth at the cut and also will help to prevent rotting.

What if i don't separate the Pups?

In nature, there is no one climbing trees and cliffs to divide the air plants (Would that qualify as a dirty job?). Because they are left alone, these tillandsias slowly start producing clumps. Overtime, large balls of air plants can cover whole tree branches and rocky protrusions. In our store, depending on availability, we sell Ionantha Balls which are clusters of Ionantha air plants that have not been separated for a few years. Natural air plant clumps produce a gorgeous flower show when in bloom!

Tips for Growing Exotic Air Plants Anywhere

Can you imagine gardening and not even having to use soil? Then, we have the plant just for you – the Tillandsias plant. This exotic plant is a member of the bromeliad family which has plants like the pineapple and other ornamental plants.

These pretty, flowering, and exotic plants are found in abundance in Central and South America without needing any soil. Tillandsias, have been coined a named called, "Air Plants" because of their lack of need for soil.

Air plants have become the "It" plants as they bring a great pop of greenery to space in fun and fashionable ways. These plants had an exotic reputation in the past, but are now known for their simple features. They can be put in almost any container because they don't need soil. This is a fun way for designers to introduce these exotic plants to every household that uses their imagination.

While these plants are very low maintenance and are great additions for indoors and outdoors don't let the nickname fool you, as these plant do need more than just air to survive. The Tillandsia plant uses the leaves to receive the adequate amount of nutrients and sunlight it needs to survive. Since these plants might be new to the average gardener, let's dive in to some basic tips for helping these exotic plants thrive in your garden.

Buy from a Nursery

When buying an air plant, you might want to consider choosing to buy from a nursery first. If you start from seed, prepare to wait a few years before you get to experience their stunning flowers. Once you have an adult plant, you can propagate them as each adult plant can have up to 12 "pups" or baby Tillandsia plants.

Get Creative with a Container

The options are endless when picking a container for these exotic plants. It was known that people were using stones, seashells, and even wood. Almost anything is going to work. The key aspect to keep in mind is that between watering the plant will have to dry out. And make sure it doesn't let the water stay inside whatever jar you want. If the tank is filled with water, make sure to drain. Even items like rope, garden tape, twist ties, and drift wood can be added to your Tillandsia plants. You can even use waterproof glue to stick them in place like liquid nails.

Water

Although these plants do not need soil, they cannot live on air alone. The Tillandsias plant needs to be irrigated on a daily basis, which is roughly two to three times a week. Air plants typically prefer to be gently misted when they are watered. If you're living in a dry environment, it's even more important to make sure you get enough water. Now, note, they're meant to dry out between every watering and there's no standing water left in the tub.

Light

The best light for your Air Plant will be in locations in your home that receive bright, but indirect light. If you are planning on usually artificial light, these plants thrive best on about 12 hours of light a day. You will notice in your plants coloring if it is receiving adequate light. The best part about these plants is that they are tiny and can be placed in unusual containers. This gives you the ability to hang in from your ceiling to make sure you plant gets the best light possible.

Temperature

The Tillandsia plant is susceptible to frost and may not do as well outdoors if you stay in a colder climate. They will live well up to 35 degrees. If you're expecting to get temperatures that are too cold, consider shielding them by covering them or taking them inside.

Fertilize

Giving your sweet little Tillandsia a nice fertilizing every month will help make sure they keep growing fast. The best months to make sure they get fertilized are March through September. When you fertilize, make sure you dilute in one-fourth intensity and try not to overdo it, you don't want to burn out the vine. There are special fertilizers that you can buy made specifically for Tillandsias.

Propagate

A Tillandsia will one bloom once in the plant's lifetime, however, they will grow "pups" which are new baby plants. One Tillandsia plant can grow up to 12 pups. If you are looking to propagate your Air Plants, you will want to cut off the offshoots, or puts that will be growing at the base of the plant. You know when it is ready to be propagated when the new Tillandsias is about half the size of the large plant.

Maintenance

If you find the blossoms of your Tillandsia have started turning yellow, go ahead and cut them off with scissors or clippers of the garden. When keeping your Air Plant looking clean and beautiful, this will help encourage new blooms.

You will note that the plant will continue to grow roots given the fact that air plants can grow without soil. They have roots to help them tie down, but they don't need them. If you find that they don't look as good or get out of control, you can cut them off. The new crop will grow as soon as possible and the plant will not be harmed.

Exotic Air Plant's Kryptonite

While adding your seed, be mindful that although they are very flexible and can be put in virtually any jar, they still have one kryptonite–copper. When they contact or are stuck to something inside it that has copper, such as pressure treated wood as it has copper and the air plant won't survive.

There really is a crop for everybody when it comes to gardening. Even if you're sure that you don't have a green thumb, you'll be able to find a plant that can help you grow. Such tropical air plants are a wonderful addition to every home and every climate. Their versatility and beautiful color can be incredible everywhere.

Keeping your Air Plants Alive

I could have cried a few years ago when I discovered my biggest, most beautiful Air Plant wilting and withering before my very eyes. It looked like it was dying! Not willing to give up on it just yet, I decided to get to the root of the problem and see if I could keep it alive. I was thrilled to find my efforts were successful!

If you're on the verge of giving up on your Air Plant, don't do it! Unless your plant falls to pieces when you pick it up or it has been exposed to freezing temperatures, some tender, loving care will likely have the plant flourishing again in no time!

Here is everything you need to know about keeping Air Plant alive, even the ones that look like they are dying! Perking your Air Plants back up is most often a quick and easy venture. In this book, you'll discover:

Reviving Your Dying Air Plant

An Air Plant that is no longer thriving "speaks to you" by displaying specific symptoms. If it is on a fast track to fatality, it may display more than one symptom. Carefully inspect the Air Plant you are concerned about. What symptoms do you see?

5 Common Symptoms of an Air Plant in Distress (and what to do about each!)

• Limpness: If your Air Plant was perky last week, but is limp today, you've caught the problem early enough to easily solve it. The problem is likely too little (or too much} light or water.

• Wilting: Leaves on an Air Plant that are wilting or curving in toward the plant's stem have either been receiving too much sunlight or not enough water. This is common if you use a spray bottle for watering, as the mist dries before the plant has been able to assimilate the water. You may want to try submerging the plant in water for about 2 hours. Also, ensure your Air Plant is receiving indirect sunlight.

• Brown Tips: This is, perhaps, the most common and frustrating "ailment" in caring for Air Plants! With sharp scissors, snip the brown tips off and double-check all the elements that work together in promoting health in Air Plants further along in this book.

• Yellow Leaves: Most often, over-watering is the culprit behind yellow(ing) leaves on an Air Plant. You may be watering too often, soaking too long, or allowing water to "pool" in the center of the plant after watering.

With-holding water for about ten days will resolve this if it is, indeed, the problem. Of course, you'll want to ensure you're following the guidelines further along in this book for proper lighting, hydration, nutrition, and protection from toxins for Air Plants.

• Leaves falling Off: This is the most critical of conditions for your Air Plant(s) to experience! If this is the issue you're facing, get the plant to a well-lit and safe location. Gently inspect the plant for any signs of a pest infestation. This is EXTREMELY rare but can happen.

Why do Air Plants Die?

Air Plants die for one of two reasons. One reason leaves you with no option for revival, and that reason is the plant has come to the end of its life cycle. This can occur between a month and a year (depending on Air Plant variety) from the time it blooms. Don't despair, though! Before the plant "officially" dies, it will produce "pups" that you can easily keep for years in your collection! You'll find more about these "pups" a little further along in this book.

The second reason that Air Plants die is that one (or more) of the elements needed to keep them alive is out of balance.

4 Things Air Plants Need to Stay Alive

It is a myth that Air Plants live on air alone! To keep your Air Plants from Dying, you must ensure all of the following elements have been addressed.

Sunlight Keeps Air Plants Alive

You'll want to display your Air Plant in a location that receives a minimum of 6 hours of bright sunlight. However, this light must be indirect or it will damage the plant.

Outdoors, this means that the Air Plant must have shelter from the sunlight. A shade tree or hanging under a porch roof are two options for displaying the plant.

Indoors, Air Plants should be in a bright room, but should only be placed directly in a window if the window isn't facing large lengths of time with direct sunlight.

In rooms that aren't brightly lit, you may want to consider artificial lighting designed to promote plant growth. I reviewed a lot of these

Proper Hydration Prevents Air Plants From Dying

If your Air Plants live outside, chances are they will only need to be watered during periods of no rain, or if you live in an extremely arid environment. Otherwise, the pant collects ambient humidity through specialized cells called Trichomes. Understand that Air Plants DO NOT collect water via their roots, like soil-dependant plants. Never soak their roots in water as a watering method!

Indoor Air Plants WILL depend on you when they're thirsty because indoor environments do not offer enough humidity for the plant to collect the water it needs.

Fertilizing Your Air Plant to Keep it Alive

Unlike plants that receive nutrient from the soil they're planted in, Air Plants gather bits of decaying plant leaves and insect matter from the atmosphere into their Trichomes and utilize that nutrition at night through the process of photosynthesis. If your Air Plant does not live outside where it can gather these nutritents, you will have to feed it by fertilization. Take caution, though! All fertilizers are NOT created equal! "Regular" plant fertilizers may contain Boron or Zinc. Both of these are toxic (and fatal) to Air Plants.

Find a fertilizer that is specially formulated for Tillandsia or Bromeliads! Because Air Plants are relatively rare in some areas, your local nursery may not offer this fertilizer. I did some looking around to save you the headache, and found a great Tillandsia fertilizer right on Amazon!

Once you've found the fertilizer that works best for your Air Plants, follow the manufacturer's instructions precisely. Too much fertilizer, as well as too little, will have a devastating outcome!

There are Toxins that will Make an Air Plant Die!

We've already gone over Boron and Zinc, two toxins commonly found in fertilizers that will kill Air Plants, but there are other toxins you should be aware of! Rust and Copper can also kill your Air Plant. Make sure that neither are present in the material of your Air Plant container or that they're not components on a display or in a terrarium.

Additionally, Air Fresheners can be toxic to your Air Plant, as well as vehicle exhaust. Give careful consideration to all things that will touch your Air Plant, and to all things in the air your Air Plant will be "breathing".

How to Water Air Plants to Keep Them Alive

The most efficient method for watering your Air Plant is by submerging it in water about every ten days. If the plant is healthy and enjoying regular and consistent watering, an hour-long soak will suffice. If the plant has shown symptoms of excessive thirst, go ahead and soak it for a couple of hours.

NOTE: Do not submerge a blossoming Air Plant. If you see evidence of a bloom beginning, or if it has already bloomed, go ahead and use the second watering method for Air Plants.

The most convenient method for watering your air Plant is misting it with a spray bottle. This is also easiest for Air Plants that are mounted to displays or mounted to wood. You'll want to mist your Air plant bout every 3 days. Should your plant show symptoms f excessive thirst even though you are misting regularly, you may want to consider submersion watering once a month or so. The reason this happens is that Air Plants cannot assimilate all the mist before it dries.

Indoors or outdoors, mist-watering or submersion, Air Plant care requires some trial and error, and adjustments as needed. What worked in the spring may not work in autumn at all! You can best "listen" to your Air Plants needs through careful observation of the plant to see if it's thriving.

Temperature and Keeping Air Plants Alive

Air plants flourish best toward the higher end of a range between 55-90 degrees Fahrenheit (12-32 Celcius). Like any living things, precautions must be taken for extreme temperatures below or above that range.

This isn't something to worry much about with indoor Air Plants, but climate should be given careful consideration when it comes to outdoor Air plants. It's rare for indoor temperatures to dip to near freezing, or to rise above the safe temperature range.

Outdoors, though, the temperatures may vary a great deal according to the season. When temperatures dip below the safe range, move your Air Plant indoors.

If your Air Plants live outside and the temperatures hit those sweltering summertime levels, be sure the plant has shade for shelter. Above that, you will want to water it more often and may want to consider adding a seasonal fertilizer as a supplement.

For temperatures that fall below the safe range, a little common sense will go a long way. Although covering the Air Plant with a sheet just as you do your "regular" plants may be helpful, the only sure way to prevent damage from the cold is to bring your Air Plant inside.

Buying Healthy Air Plants

Depending on where you live, there are three venues for acquiring an Air Plant... or several! Let's take a look at all three, knowing that likely the online option is the most popular and used method.

Buying Air Plants Online: There are a plethora of online resources for buying Air plants. I do not advocate one source over another, but there are a few things you'll want to take note of when comparison shopping. These are:

• Shipping schedule: Air Plants do ship well. I know because I've acquired some online. You'll want shipping to take no longer than three days, though, as the Air Plant will not be receiving air, moisture or nutrition during shipping.

• Cost: All online prices will vary from site to site. Consider what is included in the cost before making your final purchase decision. What is included in the higher-priced ones? A display container? Fertilizer? Multiple Air Plants? Excessive shipping fees? With some careful shopping, you can find the Air Plants that are completely within your budget!

• Will the Air Plant meet your expectations? If you're looking for a big, bold and lush Air Plant, buy it already big, bold and lush. Air Plants grow very slowly, and some will never get bigger than the palm of your hand, even fully mature. Buy the size you want, instead of waiting (and waiting) for them to grow.

• What is the Return/Refund policy of the seller? In the event that your plant arrives damaged (or worse!) will you be able to easily get your money back, or receive a replacement plant for free? You work hard for that money, protect it!

What to do When You Receive Your Beautiful Air Plants in the Mail

It's so thrilling to unpack an Air Plant when it is delivered! It's a good idea to deliver some tender loving care on delivery day to reverse any stress the shipping procedure may have caused the plant. Follow these simple steps to deliver that extra care.

1. Carefully unpack the Air Plants and all of the contents of the package.

2. Inspect the plant. Notice how it looks and feels. It should be supple without being "squishy". The Air Plant shouldn't have any brown tips or dead leaves.

3. If you do discover browning tips or any dead leaves, you can snip them off carefully with sharp scissors. If all tips are brown, and several leaves are falling off, it's time to employ that refund policy. A few needed snips are okay, though.

4. Water the Air Plant thoroughly. You'll find the methods for watering further along in this article.

5. Supplement your new Air Plant(s) with fertilizer. Be sure you only use a fertilizer formulated for Tillandsia or Bromeliads. "Regular" fertilizers may contain Zinc and/or Boron. Both of these are toxic to Air Plants! Follow instructions precisely.

6. Display your Air Plant(s) in an area that is bright, but not direct lighting. Depending on the climate where you live, your Air Plants can live outdoors or indoors. We'll take a closer look at climate today, as well.

Buying Air Plants from a Nursery or Market

If you are fortunate enough to live in a climate that supports Air Plants naturally, you'll likely find them wherever you find your soil-dependant plants. Having this "hands-on" opportunity is convenient for making sure the plant is already healthy and flourishing. Inspect the Air Plant before purchasing, and look for three things.

3 Things to look for before buying a Live Air Plant

• Supple Leaves: The leaves of the Air Plant should be soft and flexible, neither brittle nor "squishy".

• No Browing of the Leaves: Although it's normal to have an occasional brown tip or leaf, the overall condition of the plant is affected by too much browning. Air Plants are anywhere from grayish-green to yellowish-green. All brown or all yellow leaves are a RED FLAG that the plant is not healthy.

• No Leaves that are Falling Off: Again, occasionally a leaf will fall off even an Air Plant. You are looking for the "overall" condition. If several leaves fall off when you touch the plant, chances are its health has already been compromised and this is NOT the plant for you.

Best Air Plants for Your Home

Lady-Of-The-Night Orchid Air Plants

The lady-of-the-night orchid (Brassavola nodosa) is a species of the Brassavola orchids and is appropriately named for its nocturnal tendencies. This air plant is known for being easy to grow, having long-lasting inflorescences, and its nightly scent that can easily encompass a large space. The orchid has white showy flowers and an undeniable strong citrus scent, emitted in the dark hours to attract night-pollinating moths.

Vanilla Bean Orchid Air Plants

It might come to anyone as a great surprise to know that the well-loved vanilla flavor is taken from an orchid! The vanilla orchid (specifically Vanilla planifolia) is the only commercially cultivated orchid as the main source of vanillin, or the vanilla flavor. Unlike the Brassavolas, these air plants are hard to grow. The orchid grows like a vine, and its flowers only bloom for one day. However, it is still worthwhile to pursue planting it as a novelty of having your own tiny vanilla farm (although you wouldn't be harvesting and earning vanilla anytime soon with it).

Dancing Lady Orchid Air Plants

The dancing lady orchids, or the Oncidium orchids, are a group of diverse orchids, with equally diverse growing characteristics. The oncidium sharry baby is sought after because of its scent. It is said to smell like chocolate. It is also an intense smell, which might be nauseating for small rooms. If you plan to grow a fragrant air plant collection, you would be amiss to skimp over the unique choco smell of this orchid.

Lady's Slipper Orchid Air Plants

The lady's slipper orchids (Cypripedioideae) get their name from the slipper-like pouches of their flowers. These pouches serve as a catalyst for their reproduction. When insects fall inside these pouches, they are covered with pollen, thus allowing pollination to occur. A good number of these orchids aren't actually air plants and prefer the land, but some can handle being potted lightly and made into aerial plants.

Guarianthe Skinneri Air Plants

The Guarianthe skinneri is a well-known orchid in the warm areas of the US like Florida and the Gulf Coast. In fact, this orchid is actually the national flower of Costa Rica. This popular orchid has also been awarded several flower quality awards. Also, Guarianthe skinneri is fairly easy to grow, like other air plants, thus it can be the quickest addition you can make to your home.

Spider Air Plants

The spider plant (Chlorophytum comosum) is one of the easiest air plants to grow. The plant is durable, adaptable, and has a high tolerance for a wide range of conditions. The spider plant owes its name from its spiderettes, or the small plants sprouting from the mother plant. These spiderettes can become spider plants themselves, by potting them. This plant is more terrestrial than aerial, however, so taking care of it is more similar to that of plants on soil than on air.

Brachycaulos × Abdita Air Plants

This cute Tillandsia (air plants) is a hybrid of the Tillandsia brachycaulos and Tillandsia abdita. Both the brachycaulos and the abdita exhibit bright red hues in full bloom. It wouldn't be the strangest thing for their hybrid to produce vivid red and pink inflorescences in their prime. These species are both highly coveted due to their significant shift of hue from growth to bloom. You would be missing out on your collection if you would miss either of the species or their hybrid. They are also relatively simple to take care, so there's nothing else to fuss over.

Tillandsia Xerographica Air Plants

Tillandsia xerographicas would make for excellent hanging air plants. With its long tapering leaves waving below its own base, it forms a tight rosette. You will hear much about this huge Tillandsia for its full and spherical shape. You can thank it for its leaves' wavy burst then fall from its center. Its curls at the tips of its leaves and the magnificence of its rosette base are its charms. These make it all the reason to put these air plants in your home as part of your indoor garden!

Tillandsia Tectorum Ecuador Air Plants

Requiring the most minimal of care, the T. tectorum ecuador is a furry little addition to your air plants. Gathering from its name, this tiny one hails from the warm, warm lands of Peru and Ecuador. This plant has developed a frugal use of these nutrients as one of its adapting mechanisms, with its excessive trichomes. Because of this, this plant falls under the beginner box for not needing to be watered as much as the others. In fact, there are more not-to-dos than to-dos in taking care of this little fellow!

Tillandsia Stricta Air Plants

Tillandsia stricta flowers can be considered a relative rarity. It is due to the fact that T. stricta only blooms once. To make up for it, the flowers last longer. Common to all Tillandsias is that these air plants also require very little maintenance. After blooming, "pups" grow from under the flower.You can take the pups off when they reached a third of their mother plant's size and let them grow independently. You can also let them be. In doing so, the Tillandsia will then eventually form a clump.

Tillandsia Ionantha Air Plants

The T. ionantha air plant is definitely one of the most popular of the air plants. A large variety of ionanthas serve as a standing proof of its fame. They are also popular because they are very easy to take care of. The growth cycle of the ionanthas start with green and silver-hued leaves. Over time, the leaves extend outward as their green hue becomes darker. When the blooming phase commences, the leaves create a red and pink gradient together with the greens.

Tillandsia Funkiana Air Plants

Tillandsia funkiana air plants resemble a caterpillar, a cactus, or a pine tree rather than anything else. But you would be wrong to think that it's sharp because these leaves are actually soft. The plant is also hardy, making it a beginner-friendly Tillandsia. It grows on a stem and exhibits lightly-colored greens, making it a beautiful accent anywhere in the home. It also clusters very well.

Tillandsia Bulbosa Air Plants

These Tillandsia bulbosa air plants can cast creepy shadows in the night. With its long-winding arms reminiscent of snakes or tentacles, it would be more scary than beautiful if not for its Tillandsianess. In the bright light, the bulbosa is a tiny beauty to behold. Its flat leaves form the eponymous bulb, where the arms also come from. As with most Tillandsias, the bulbosa is a breeze to take care of. Any newcomer to the business would easily welcome themselves into this happy world using these air plants.

Tillandsia Aeranthos Air Plants

The Tillandsia aeranthos is best friends with the hummingbird in its natural habitat. The latter is responsible for its pollination. It has stiff green leaves which point upward to their light source. In bloom, their flowers are pretty in their pink hues, dabbled with beautiful purple ones later on in the season. You can also remove the growing pups and let them grow independently or leave them be to form a clump. Either way, the aeranthos and all its varieties are easy air plants to take care of.

Tillandsia Caput-Medusae Air Plants

It goes by the common name octopus plant or medusa's head, and rightfully so for either. With its pseudobulb and its outstretched arms, it would be no wonder to mistake it as either. But nevertheless, these air plants maintain all common characteristics of Tillandsias. It is a beginner-friendly plant, can be formed individually or into clumps, and has trichomes which help it in taking in nutrients. It can also be planted in rocks as an aesthetic choice.

How to Display Your Air Plants

There is no limit to the creative ways to view air plants in your home, as described above. But in order to ensure proper care, there are a few things to know about presenting.

On a bookshelf or coffee table, a Tillandsia show in a terrarium or glass bowl can look amazing. If the bowl's mouth helps you to remove the soaking seed, continue the above process. Keep in mind that a bowl or terrarium provides a more moist micro-climate and may require less watering. It is best not to put a glass container right on a windowsill as glass intensifies the heat of the sun and burns the seed!

If air plants cannot be removed from their glass home due to scale, it is only fitting to water the air plant by foaming. But because the plant requires air circulation, the smaller the jar, the longer it will dry out. Less frequent watering is required. Larger glass containers should have more air circulation, and they should be misted more frequently.

For air plants which are mounted on walls or glued to wood or other mediums, misting rather than soaking will be required. Remember to mist all around the plant, rather than on the plant, as this will create a humid environment.

Air Plants Pests

The indoor air plant that has spent its life at very low risk of attracting the bugs that may be found in other indoor plants. Obviously, having no soil means that Tillandsia is not affected by pests growing in the soil.

Bugs like aphids or mealybugs on an air plant are not difficult to see; in this case, a good soak or, if necessary, a sprinkle of Diatomaceous Earth will solve the problem.

CONCLUSION

The advantages of air plants are enormous and indispensible. You will maximize your health benefits and lead a life of fulfillment. Every day, you're going to be happy and surrounded by positivity. You're going to look amazing and feel fantastic from the depths of your hands. We contribute to the overall well-being of the individual. In addition, you want the air plants to make your house stand out. They will enrich the color and design of your already enticing house. Grow your air plants and get the most out of them.

Not everybody has a green thumb so that a tree can grow from a seed. But that doesn't stop anyone wanting to be able to do that. Air plants are the place where we can wet our feet with the thought of growing a crop, with the ease of setting it up and taking care of it. Usually, almost everyone can try air plants at low dirt prices and even use them to relieve pain or to make tea with a little care. Whether you want to dabble in gardening, these plants are a really good fit for you. Even if you decide midway to give up the idea, you can still keep the plant and feel almost no change in your lifestyle, except the calming sight of green and floral colors ripping the ire-inspiring grey fabric of every day.